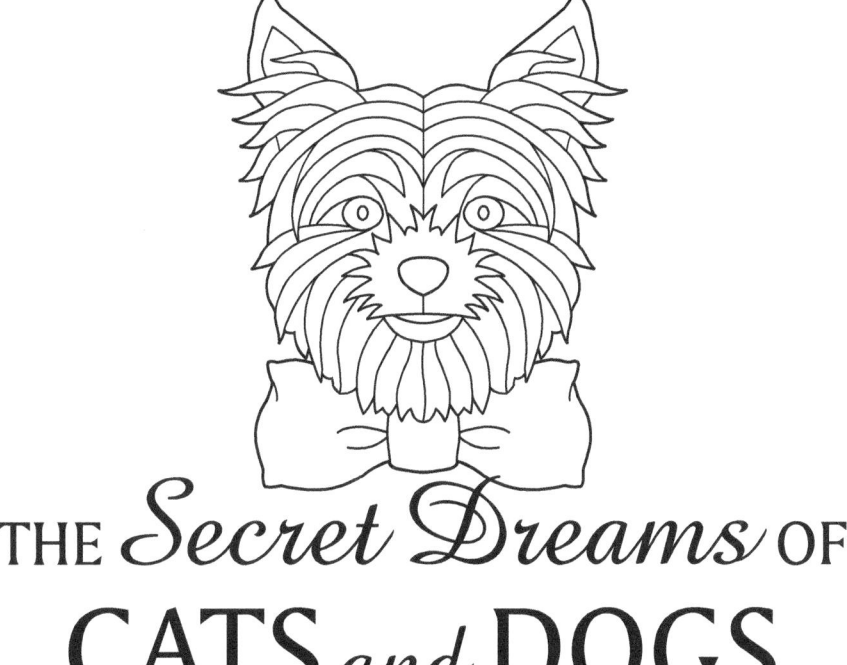

THE *Secret Dreams* OF CATS and DOGS

A Creative Coloring Book for Dreamers

By Katherine DeVault

TABLE OF CONTENTS

Cats Who Dream

Dogs Who Dream

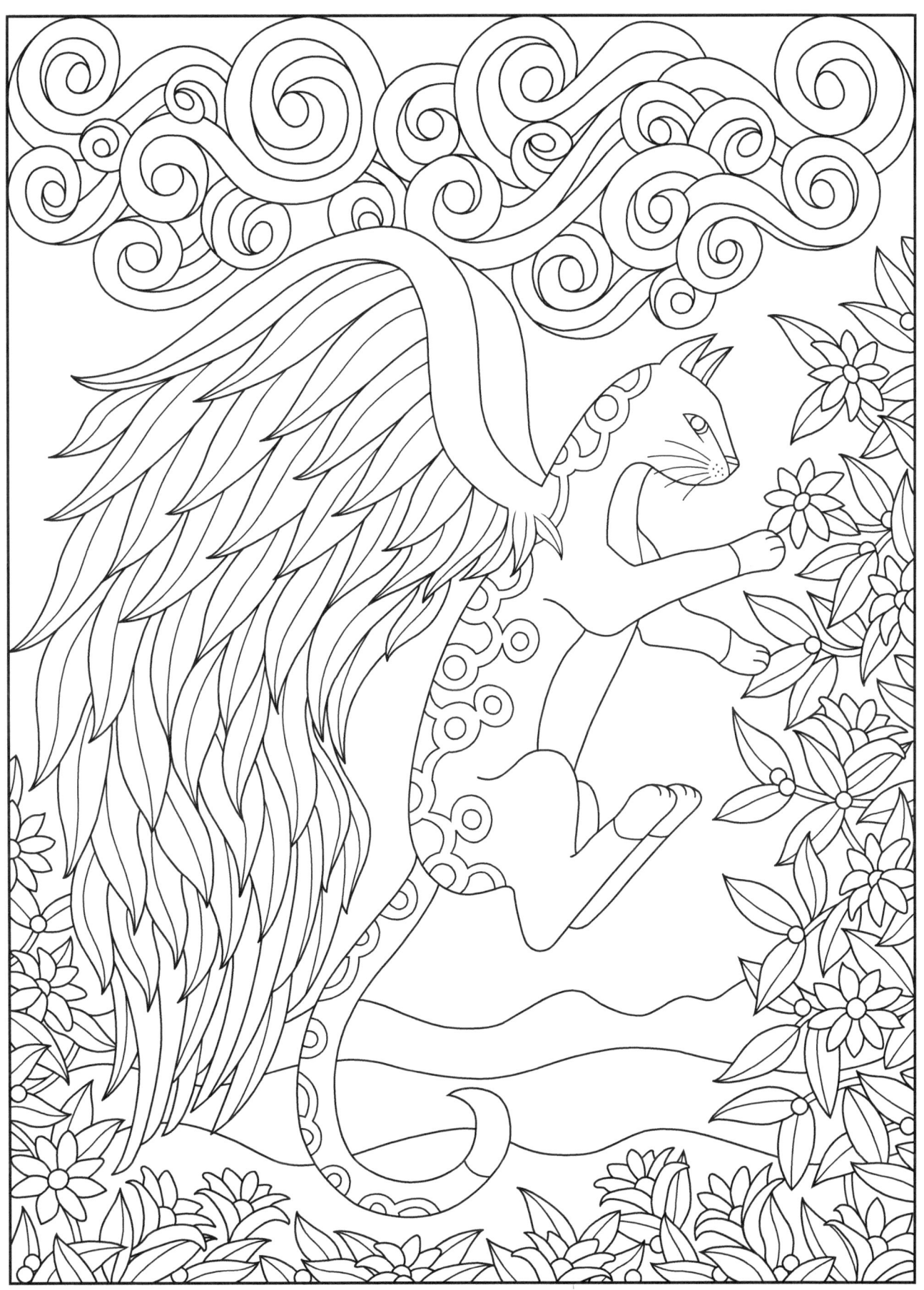

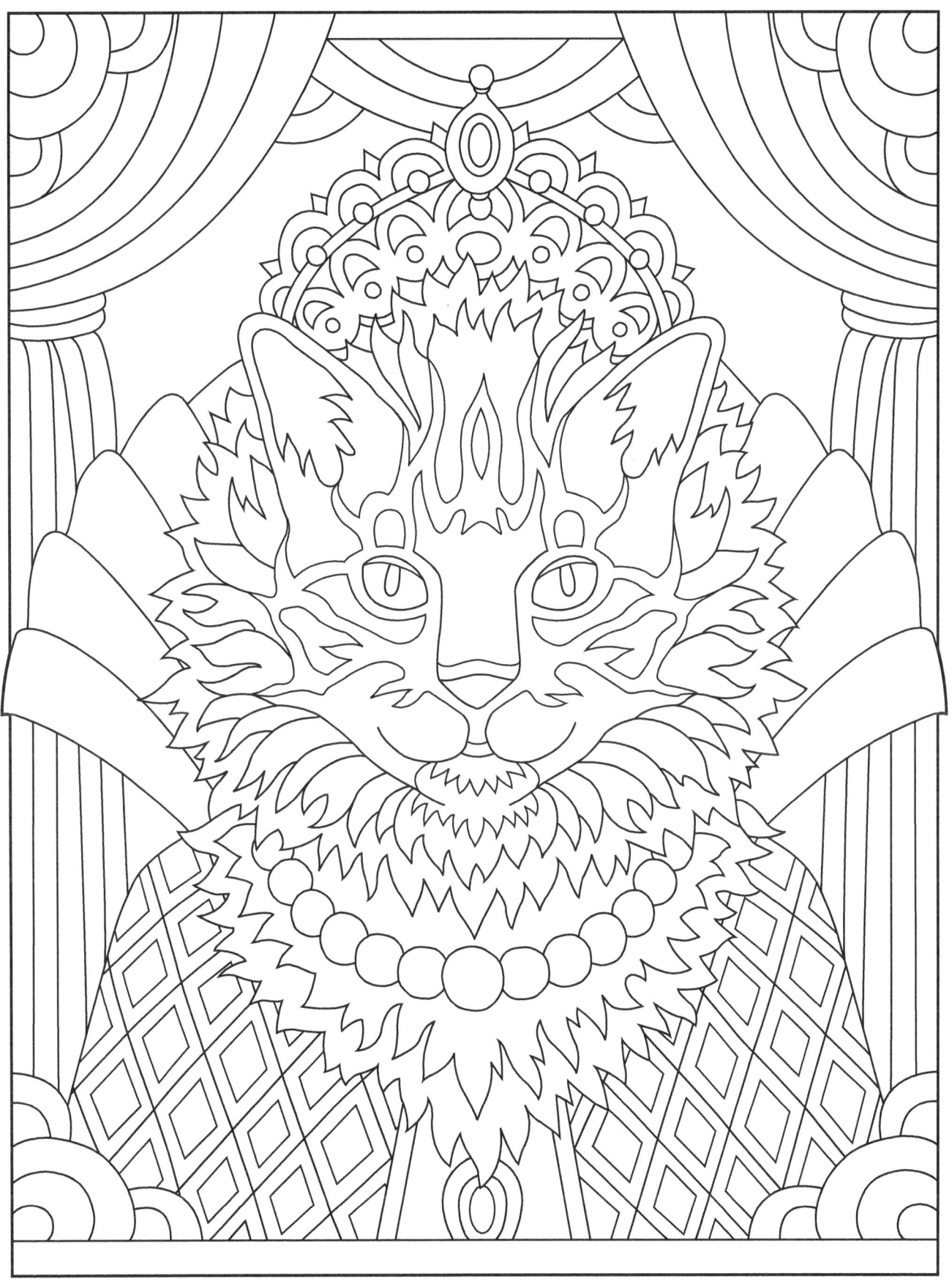

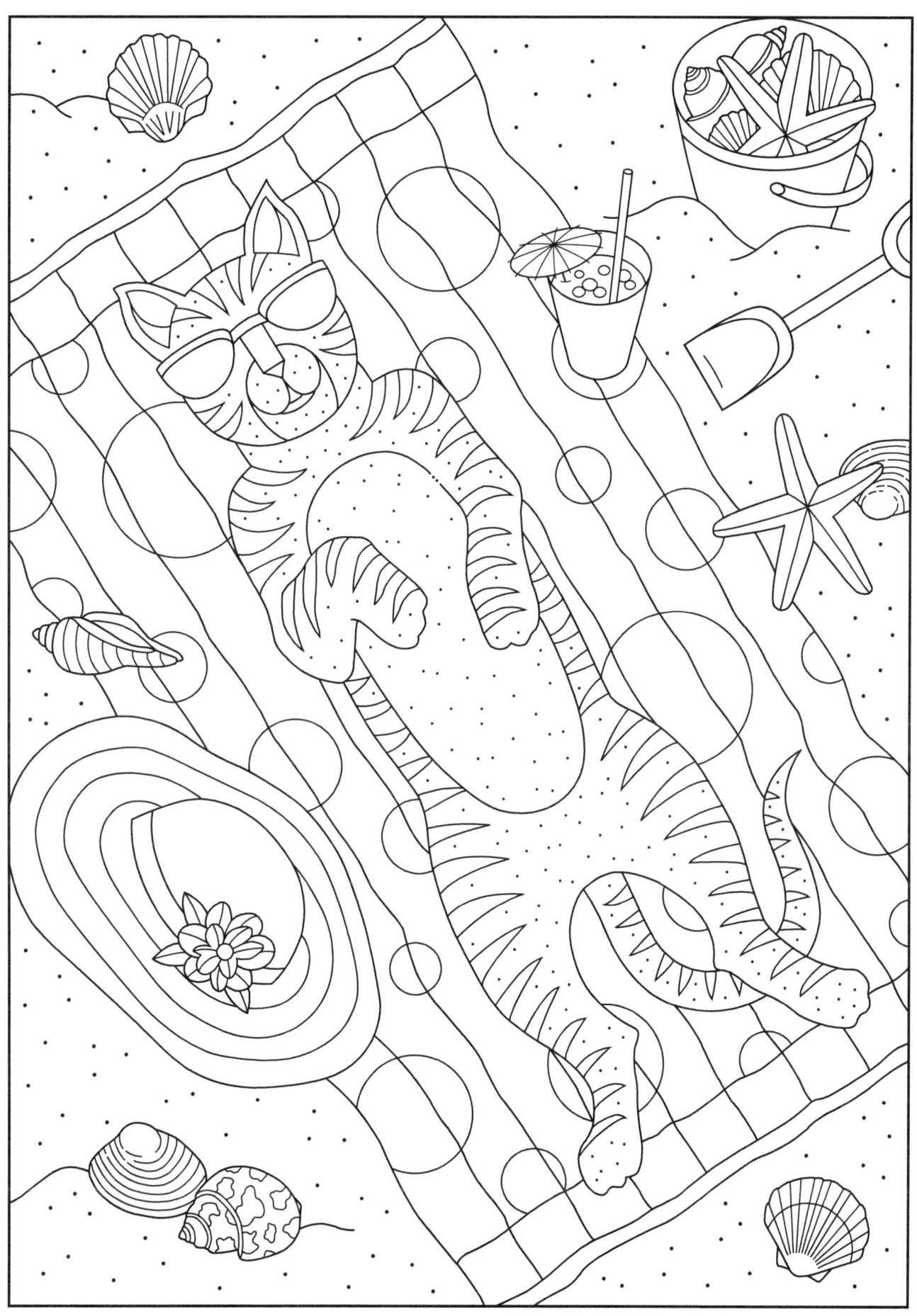

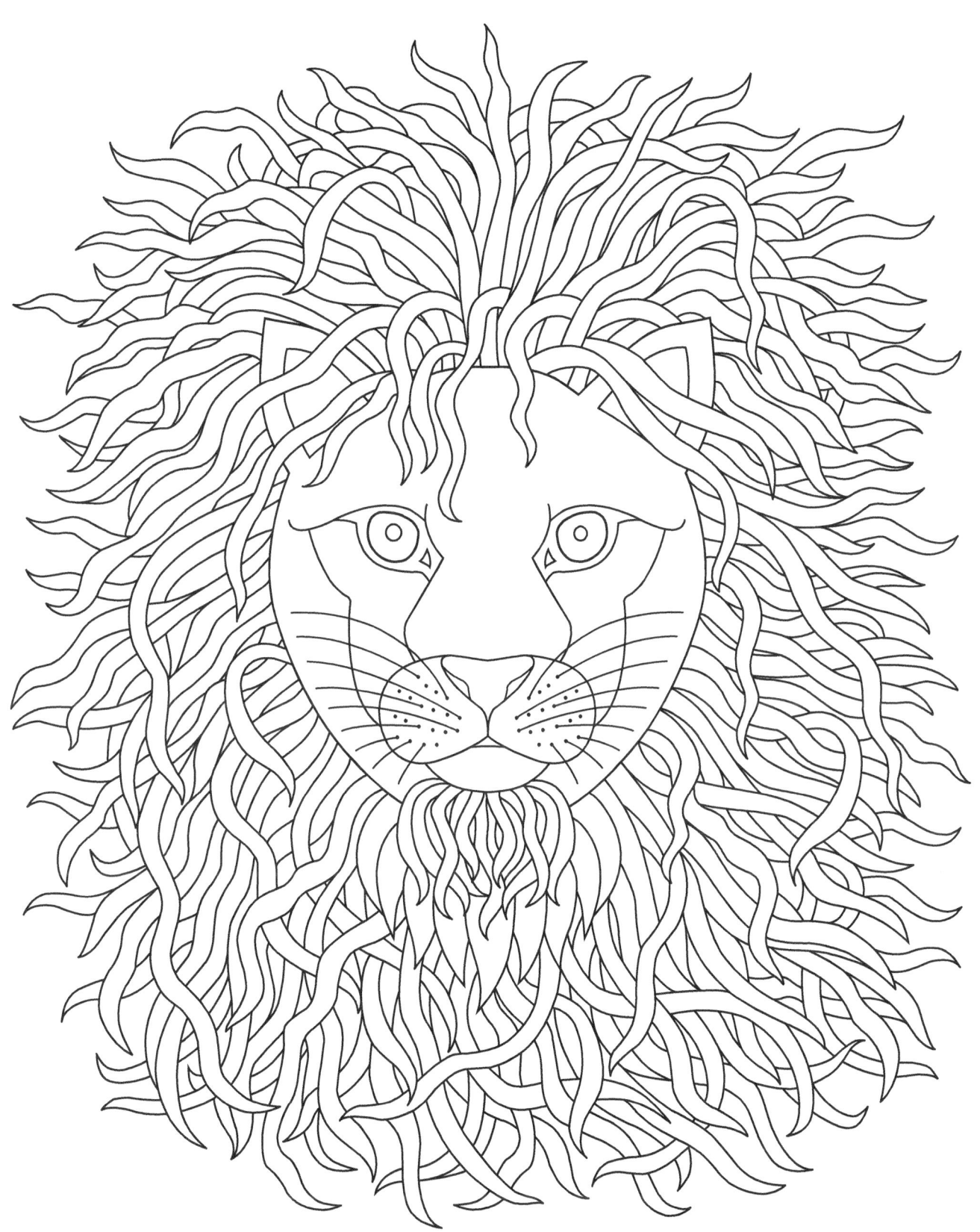

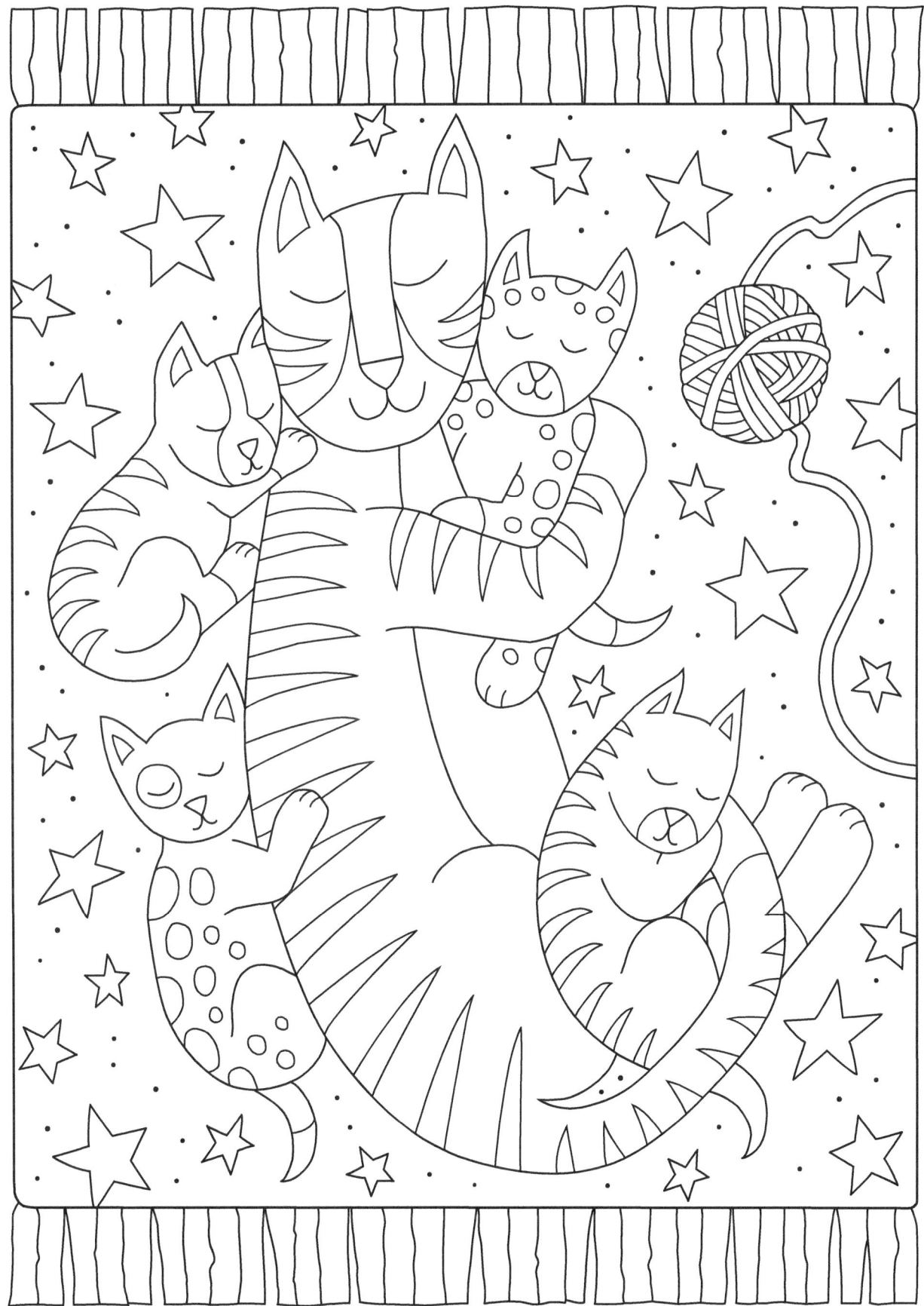

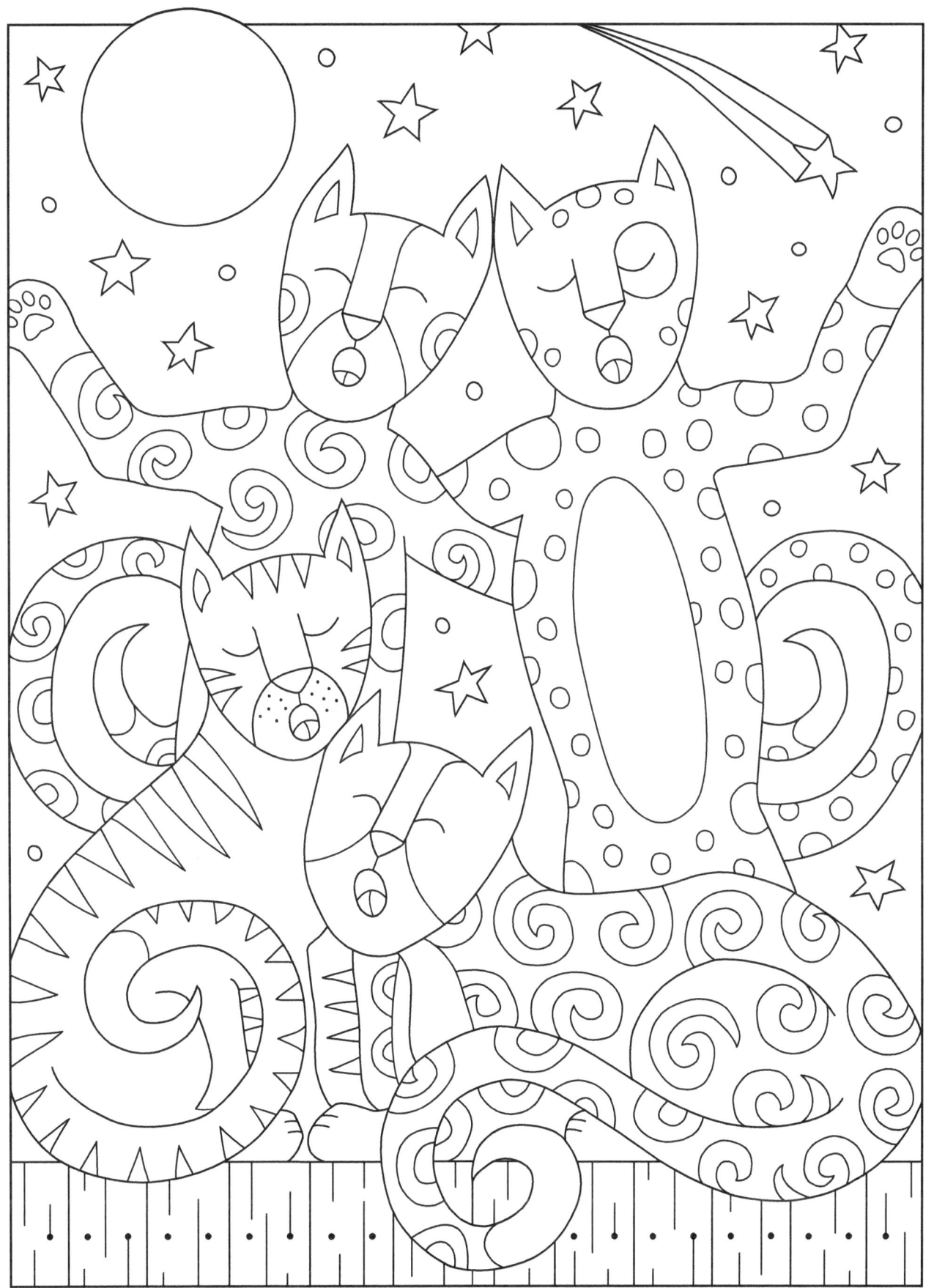

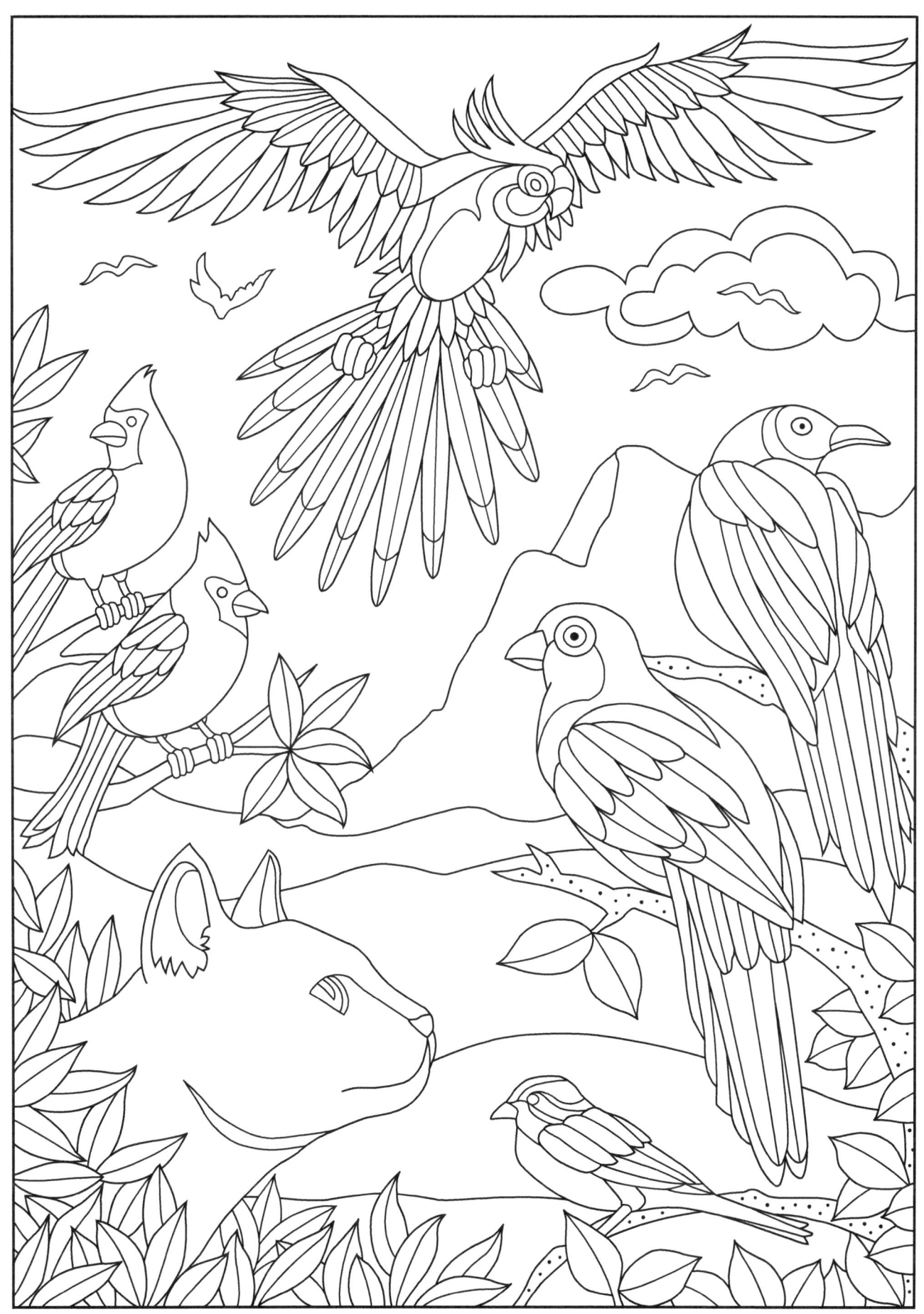

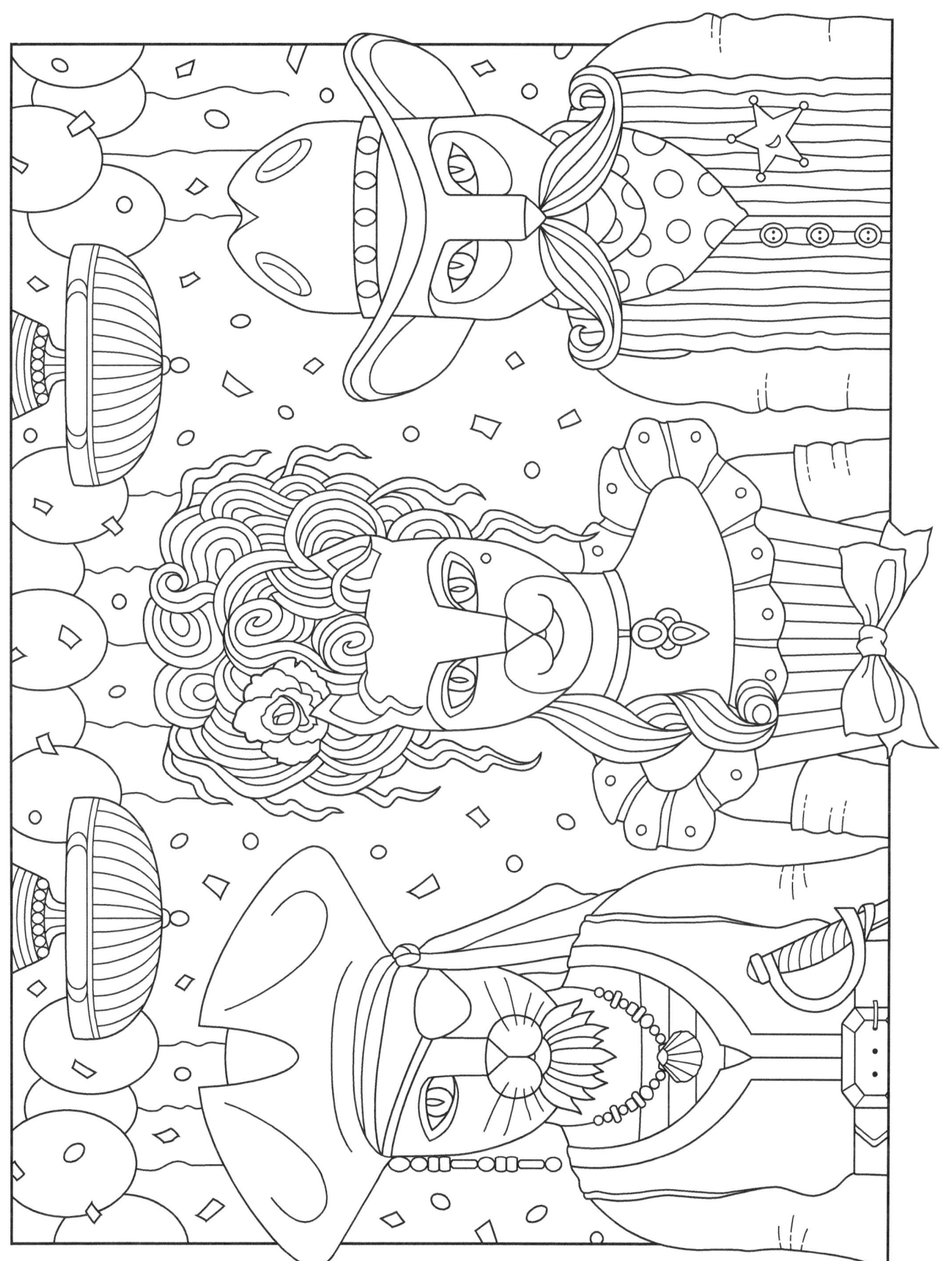

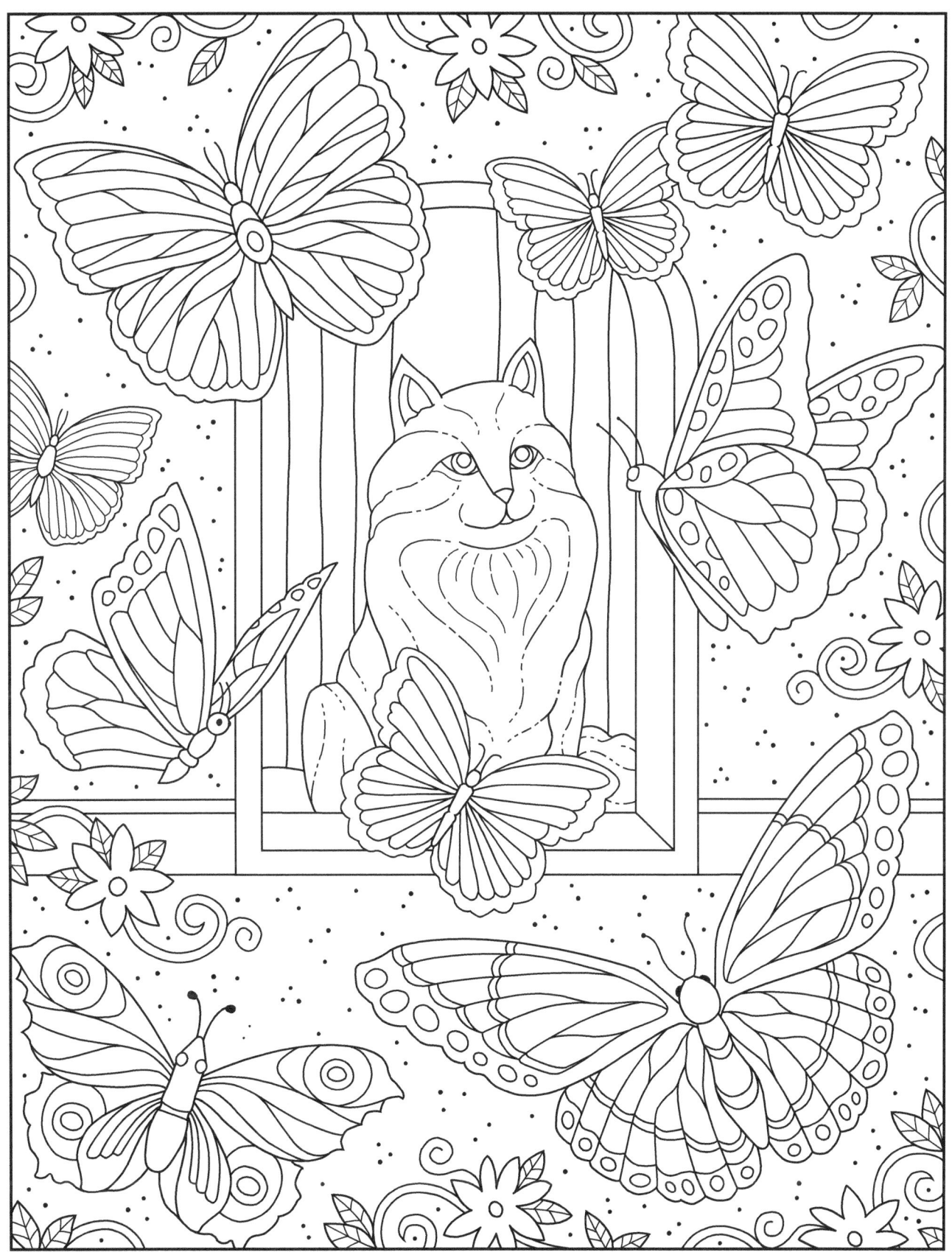

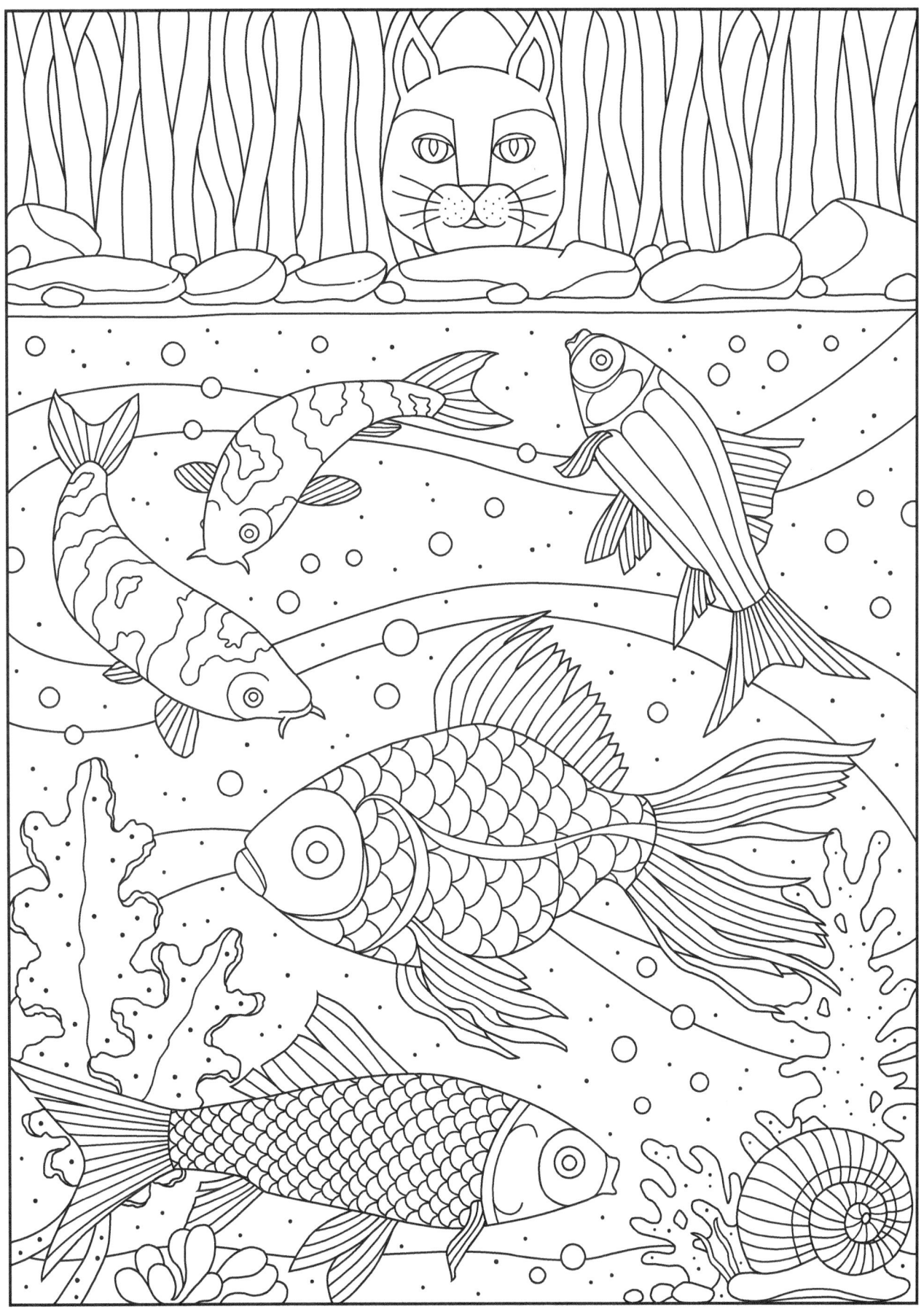

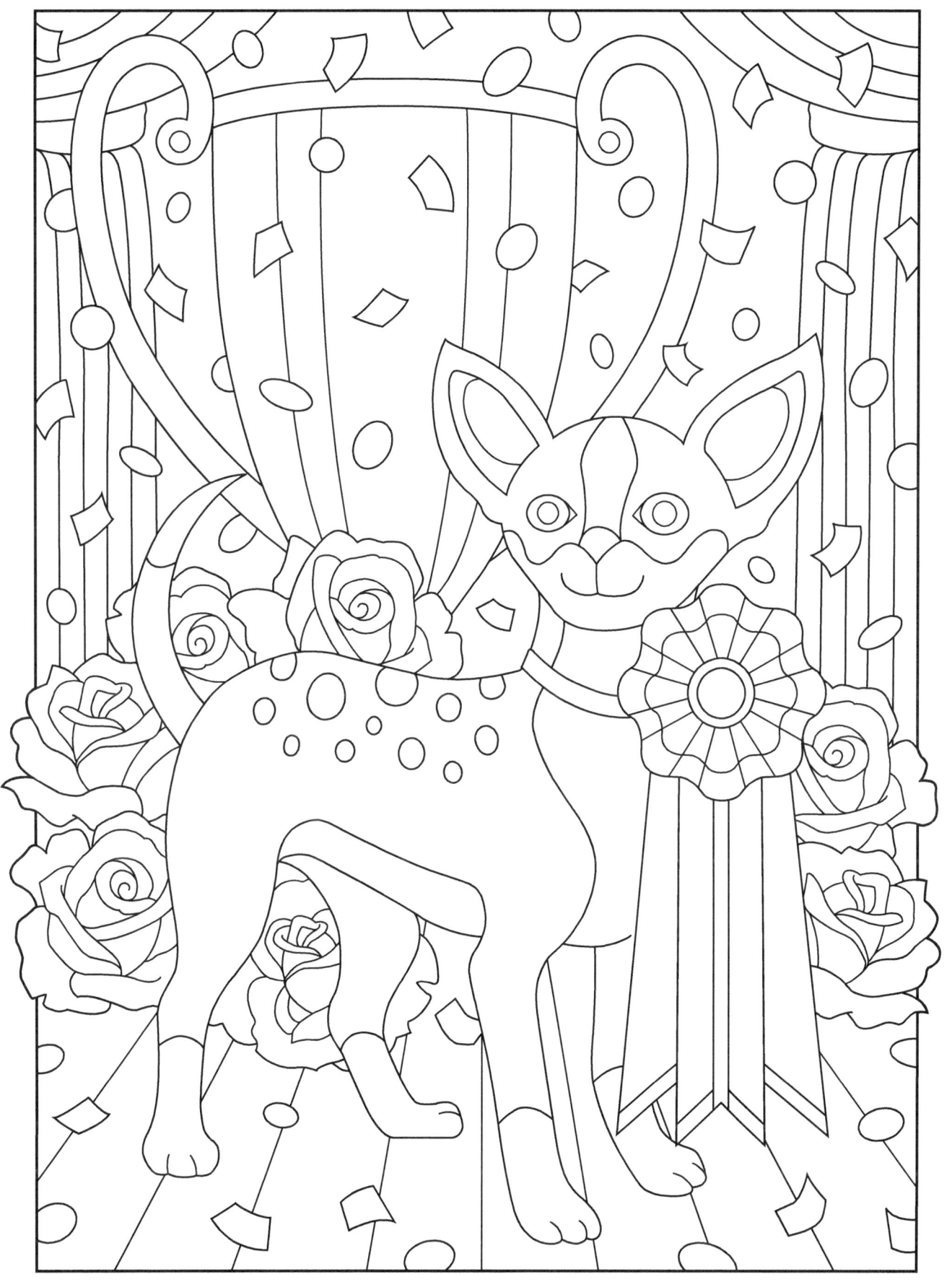

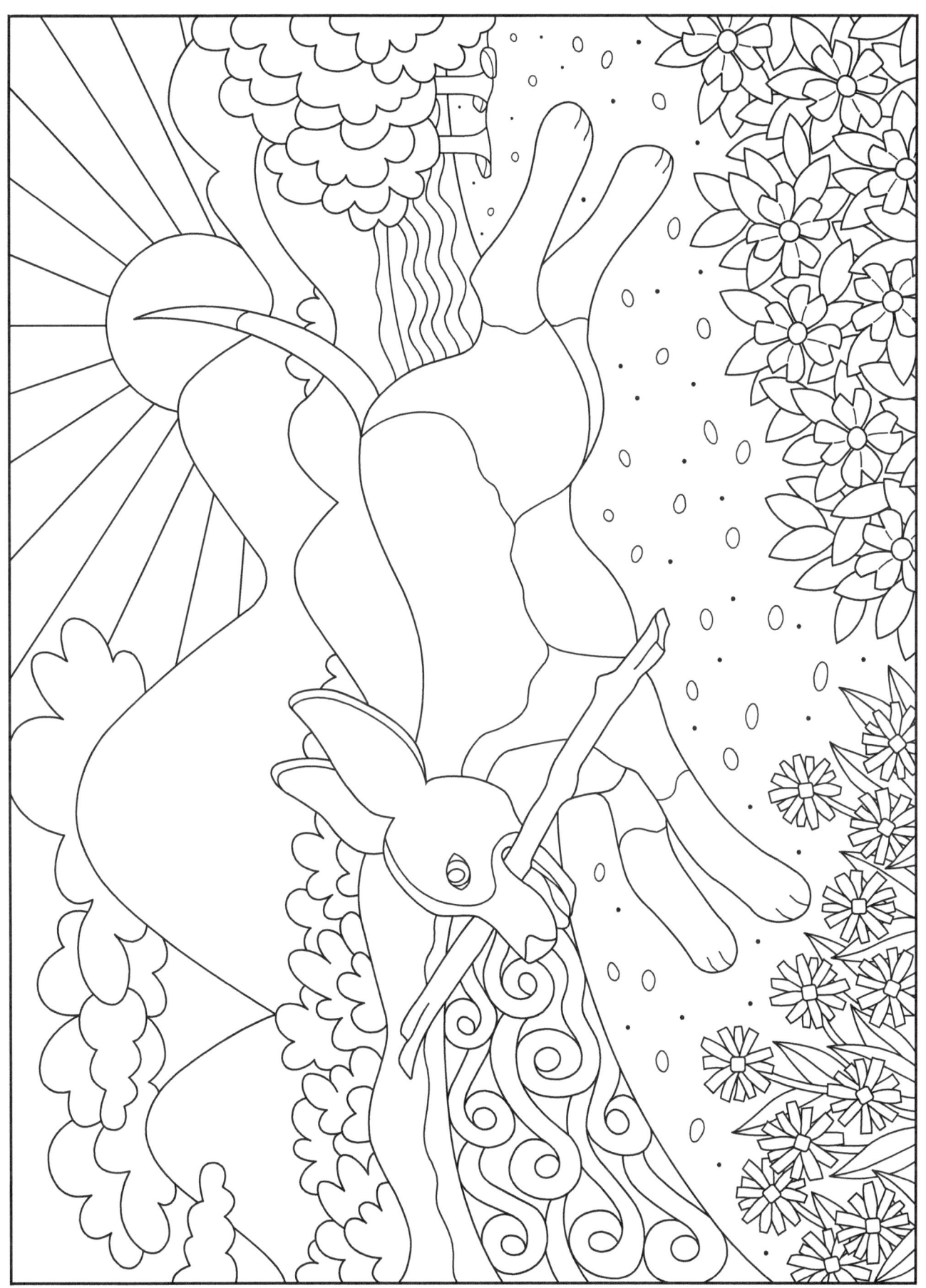

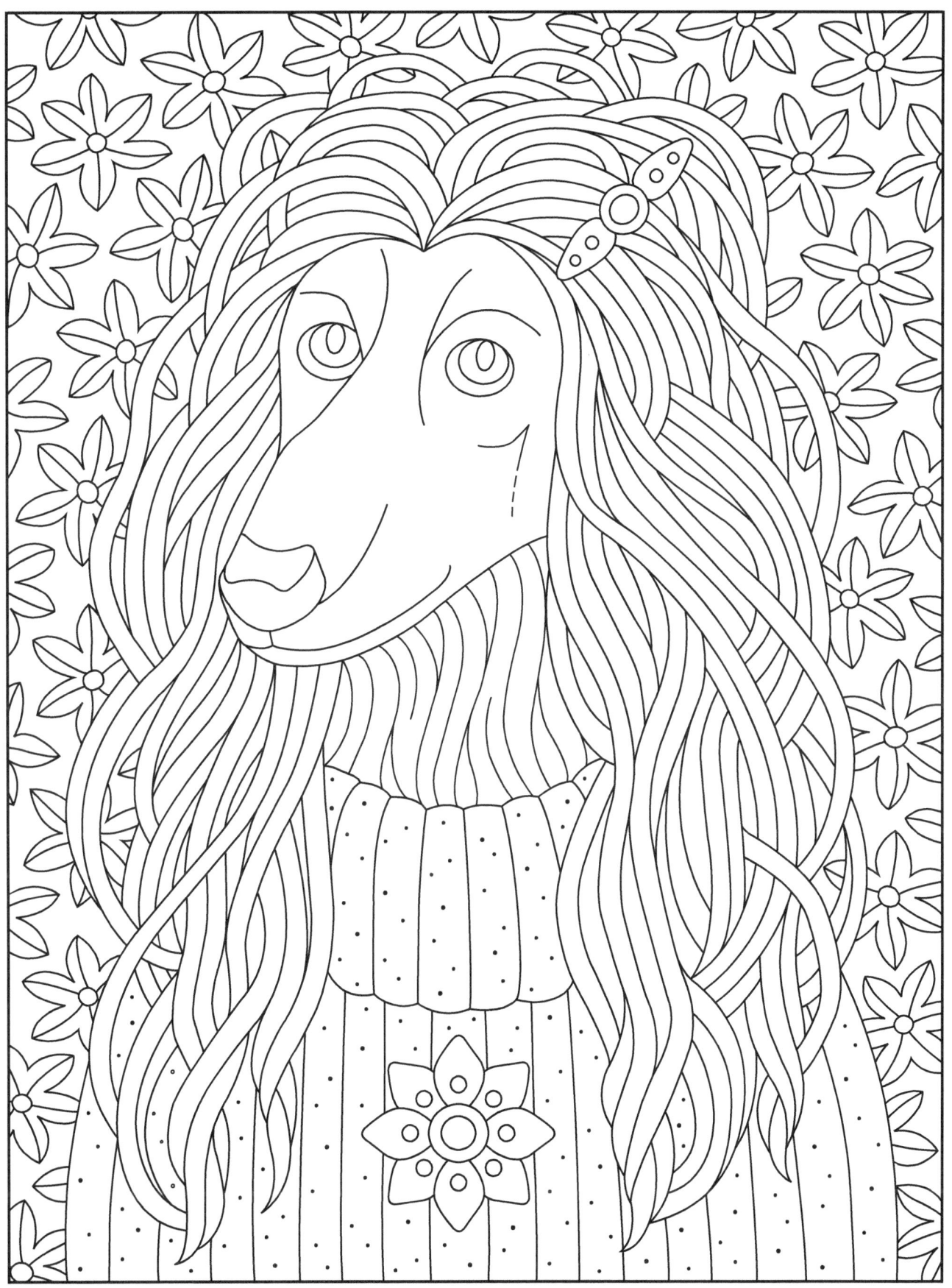

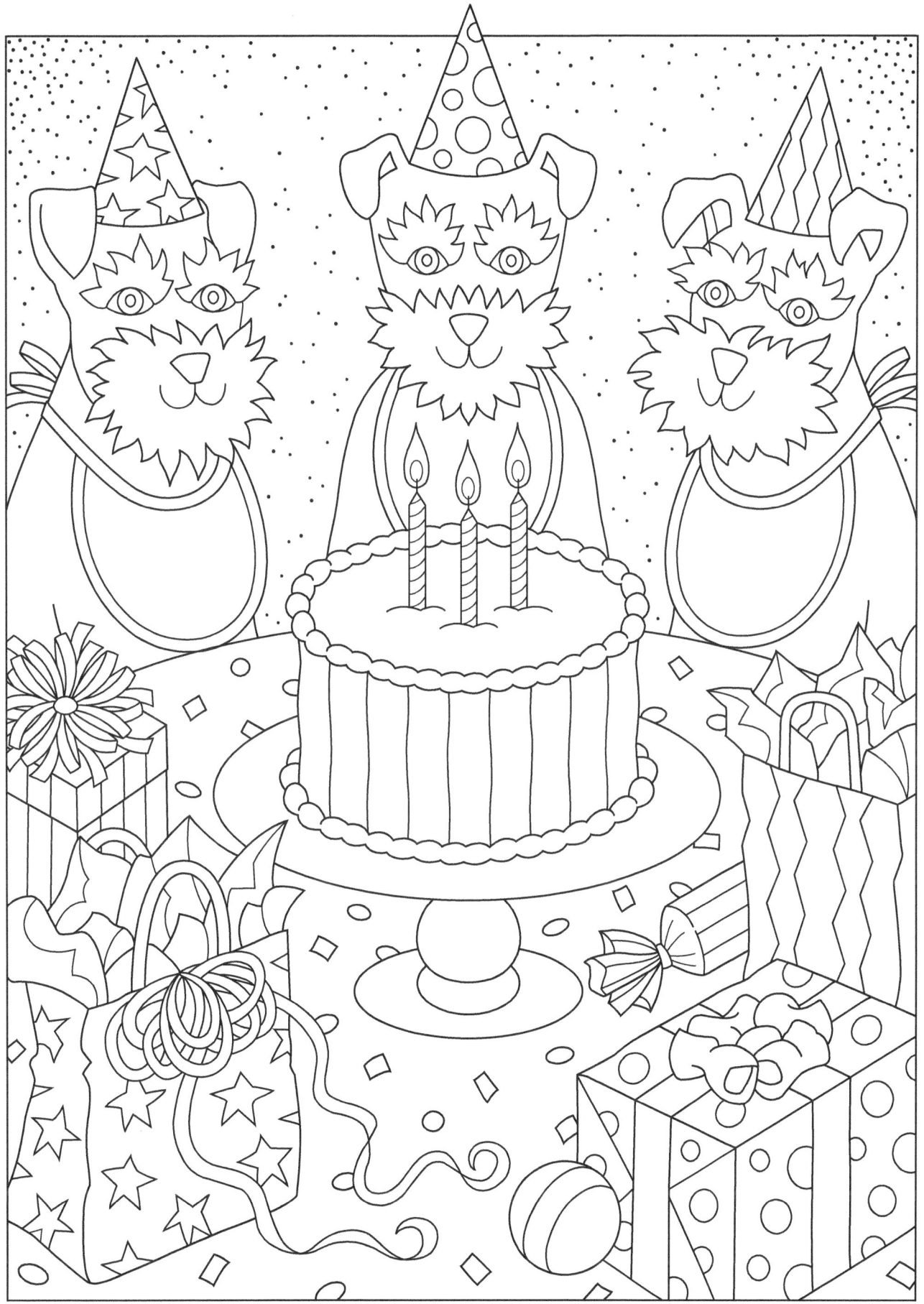

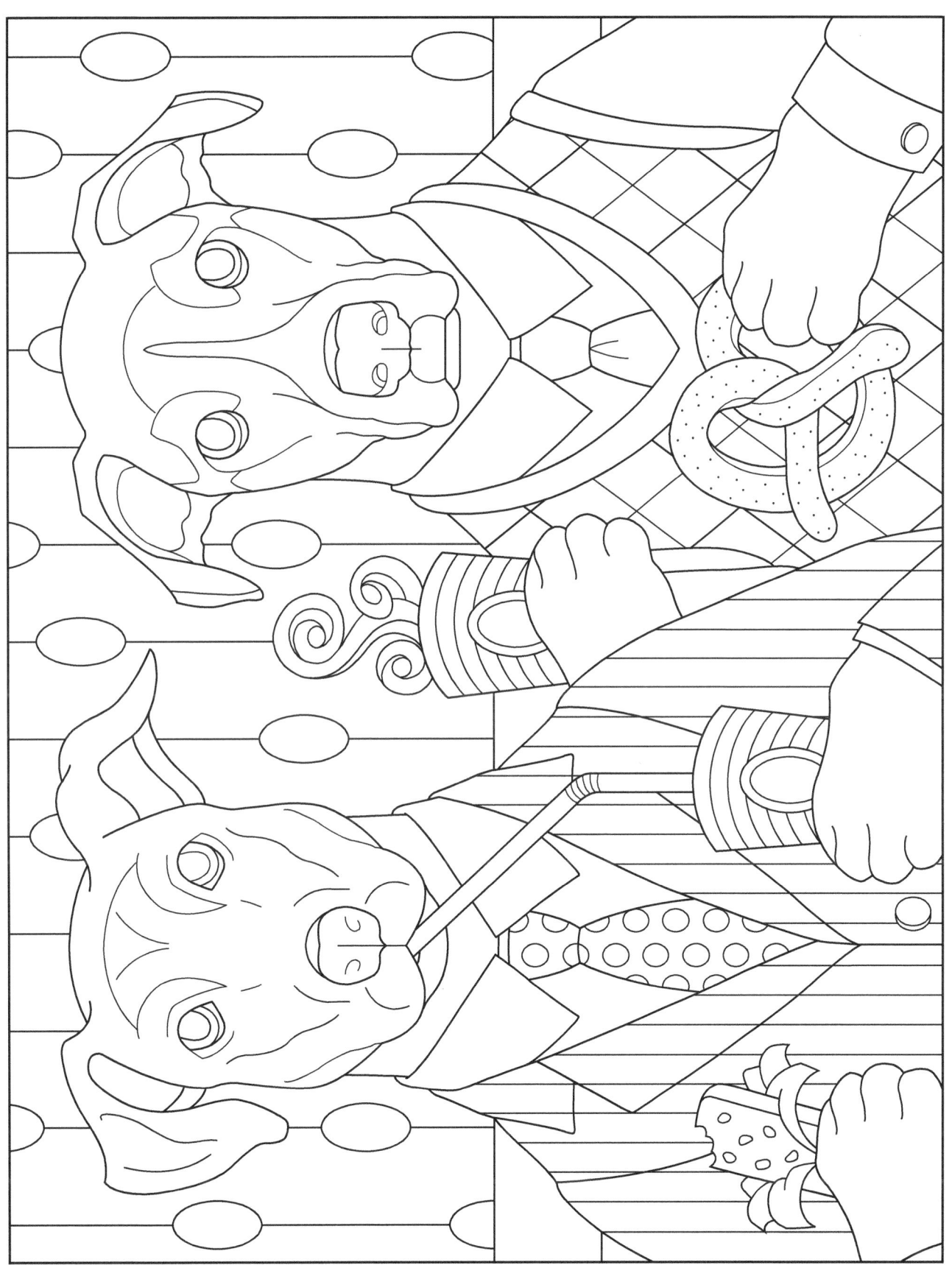

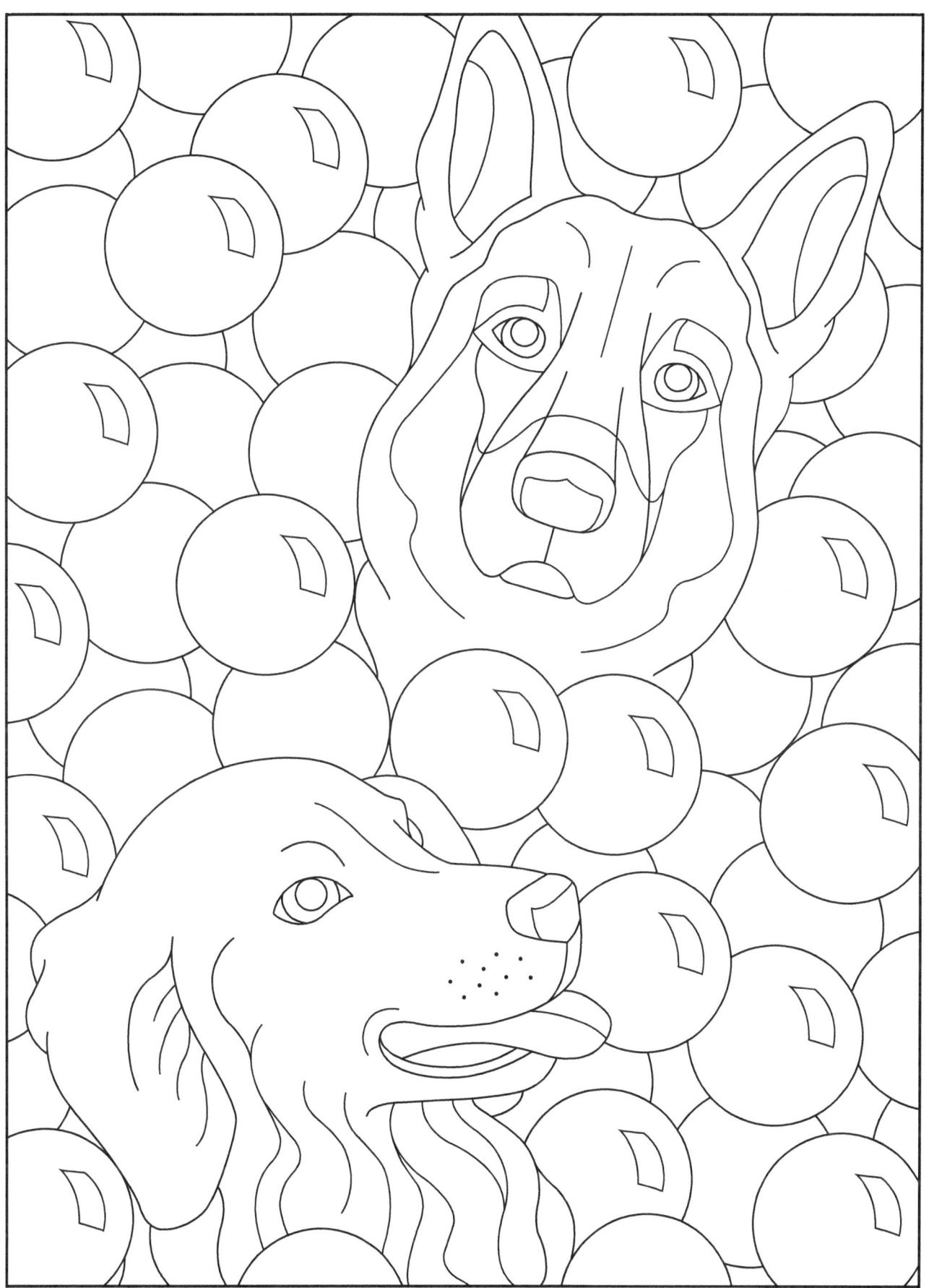

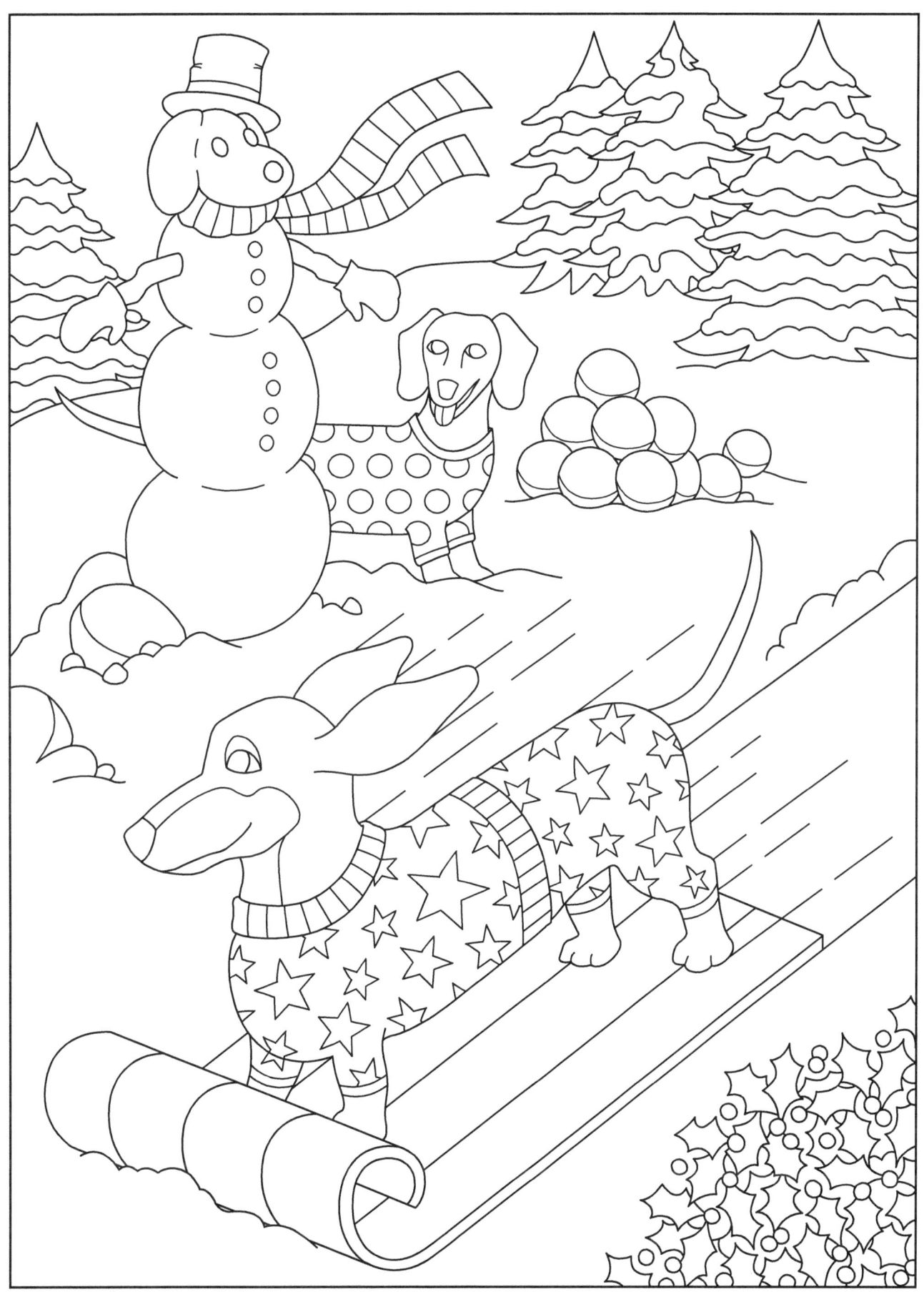

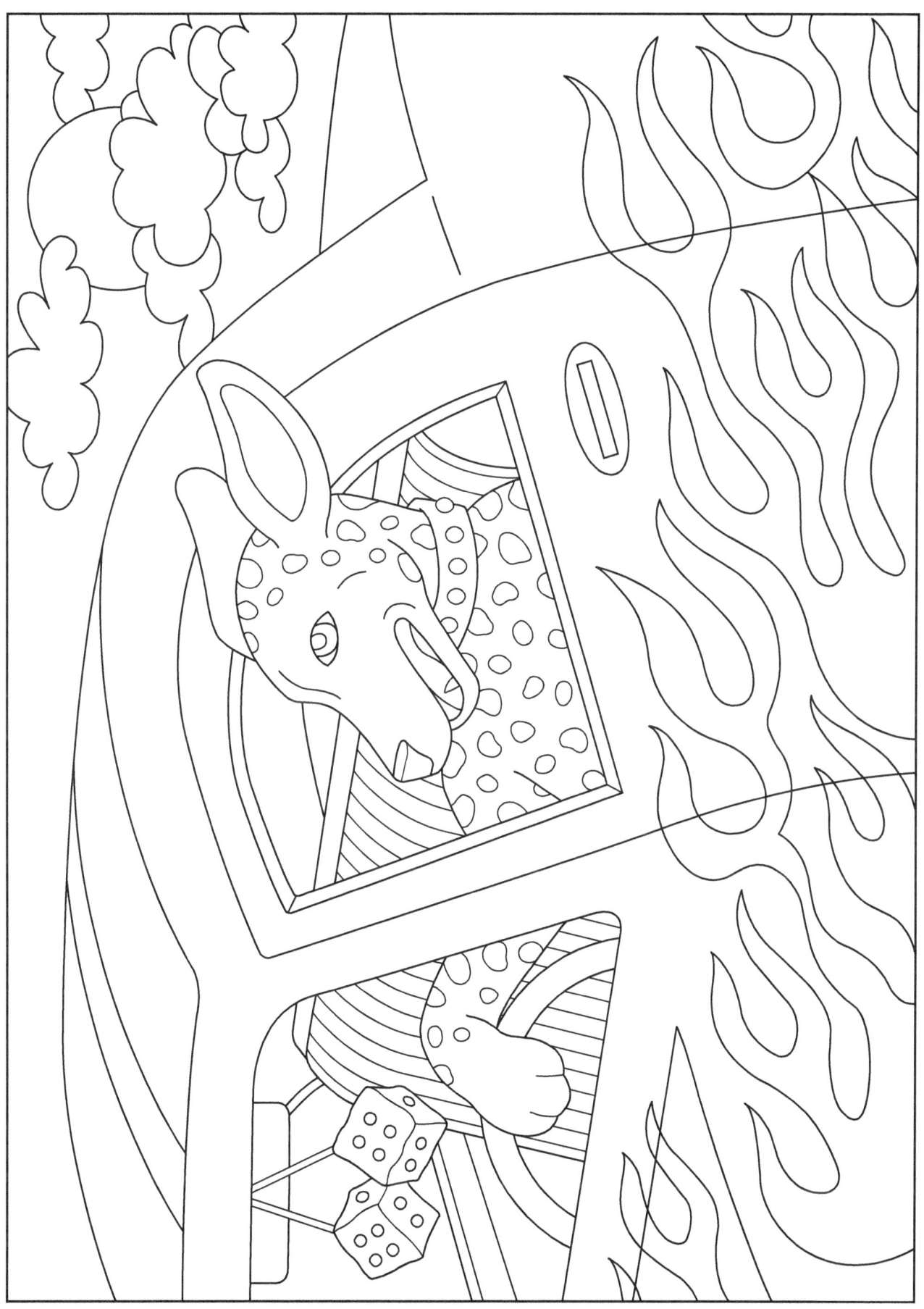

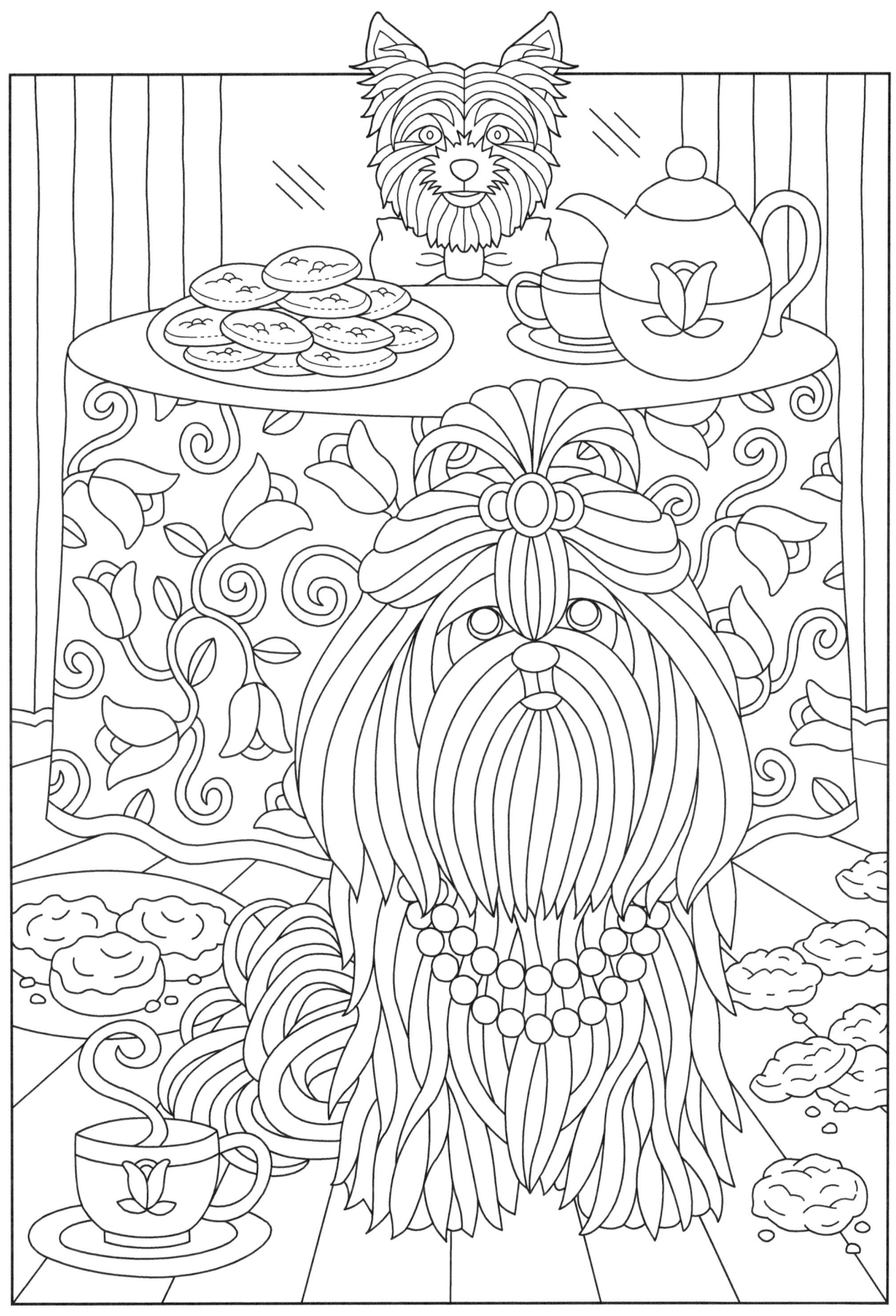

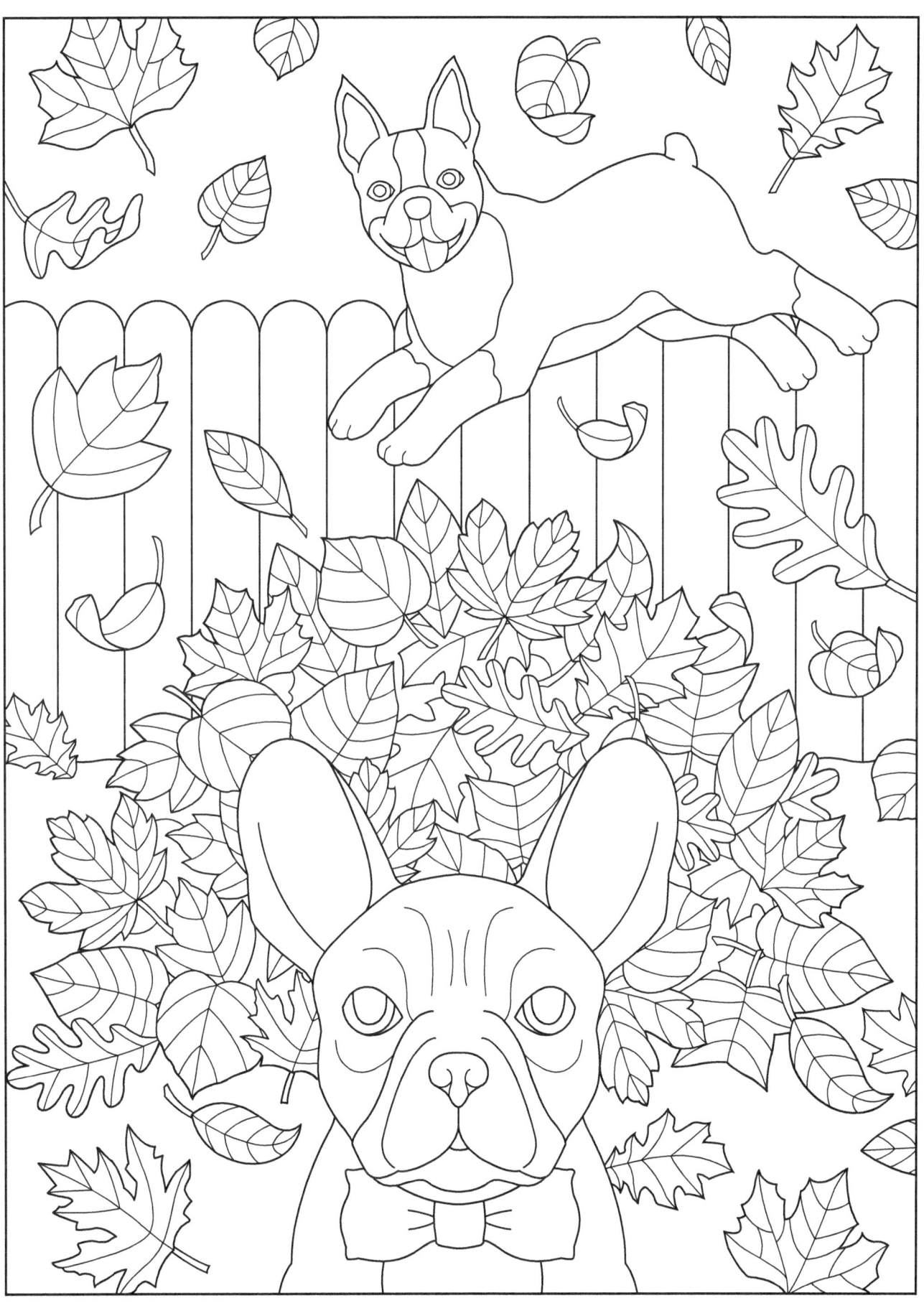

www.ingramcontent.com/pod-product-compliance
Lightning Source LLC
Chambersburg PA
CBHW081802170526
45167CB00008B/3297